GW00721958

FRANCIS FRITH'S

SOUTHWOLD TO ALDEBURGH

PHOTOGRAPHIC MEMORIES

CAROL AND MICHAEL WEAVER are history teachers at Woodbridge School, and this is their second Frith volume. Poised on the brink of retirement, they hope to use both books to show their newly arrived grandson, Archie, the delights of this part of Suffolk when he is old enough. Meanwhile they dedicate their efforts to Doreen Weaver, 1919-2004, whose encouraging phrase, 'one last effort', seems to have worked yet again.

FRANCIS FRITH'S
PHOTOGRAPHIC MEMORIES

SOUTHWOLD TO ALDEBURGH

PHOTOGRAPHIC MEMORIES

CAROL AND MICHAEL WEAVER

First published in the United Kingdom in 2004 by
Frith Book Company Ltd

Limited Hardback Subscribers Edition Published in 2004
ISBN 1-85937-847-1

Paperback Edition 2004
ISBN 1-85937-848-X

British Library Cataloguing in Publication Data

Francis Frith's Southwold to Aldeburgh - Photographic Memories
Carol and Michael Weaver

Frith Book Company Ltd
Frith's Barn, Teffont,
Salisbury, Wiltshire SP3 5QP
Tel: +44 (0) 1722 716 376
Email: info@francisfrith.co.uk
www.francisfrith.co.uk

Printed and bound in Great Britain

Front Cover: **SOUTHWOLD**, *The Beach 1919* 69118
Frontispiece: **SOUTHWOLD**, *The Beach 1906* 56834

*The colour-tinting is for illustrative purposes only, and is not intended
to be historically accurate*

AS WITH ANY HISTORICAL DATABASE THE FRITH ARCHIVE IS
CONSTANTLY BEING CORRECTED AND IMPROVED AND THE
PUBLISHERS WOULD WELCOME INFORMATION ON OMISSIONS OR
INACCURACIES

CONTENTS

FRANCIS FRITH
VICTORIAN PIONEER

FRANCIS FRITH, founder of the world-famous photographic archive, was a complex and multi-talented man. A devout Quaker and a highly successful Victorian businessman, he was philosophical by nature and pioneering in outlook.

By 1855 he had already established a wholesale grocery business in Liverpool, and sold it for the astonishing sum of £200,000, which is the equivalent today of over £15,000,000. Now a very rich man, he was able to indulge his passion for travel. As a child he had pored over travel books written by early explorers, and his fancy and imagination had been stirred by family holidays to the sublime mountain regions of Wales and Scotland. 'What lands of spirit-stirring and enriching scenes and places!' he had written. He was to return to these scenes of grandeur in later years to 'recapture the thousands of vivid and tender memories', but with a different purpose. Now in his thirties, and captivated by the new science of photography, Frith set out on a series of pioneering journeys up the Nile and to the

Near East that occupied him from 1856 until 1860.

INTRIGUE AND EXPLORATION

These far-flung journeys were packed with intrigue and adventure. In his life story, written when he was sixty-three, Frith tells of being held captive by bandits, and of fighting 'an awful midnight battle to the very point of surrender with a deadly pack of hungry, wild dogs'. Wearing flowing Arab costume, Frith arrived at Akaba by camel sixty years before Lawrence of Arabia, where he encountered 'desert princes and rival sheikhs, blazing with jewel-hilted swords'.

He was the first photographer to venture beyond the sixth cataract of the Nile. Africa was still the mysterious 'Dark Continent', and Stanley and Livingstone's historic meeting was a decade into the future. The conditions for picture taking confound belief. He laboured for hours in his wicker dark-room in the sweltering heat of the desert, while the volatile chemicals fizzed dangerously in their trays. Back in London he exhibited his photographs and was 'rapturously cheered' by members of the Royal Society. His reputation as a photographer was made overnight.

VENTURE OF A LIFE-TIME

Characteristically, Frith quickly spotted the opportunity to create a new business as a specialist publisher of photographs. He lived in an era of immense and sometimes violent change.

For the poor in the early part of Victoria's reign work was exhausting and the hours long, and people had precious little free time to enjoy themselves. Most had no transport other than a cart or gig at their disposal, and rarely travelled far beyond the boundaries of their own town or village. However, by the 1870s the railways had threaded their way across the country, and Bank Holidays and half-day Saturdays had been made obligatory by Act of Parliament. All of a sudden the working man and his family were able to enjoy days out and see a little more of the world.

With typical business acumen, Francis Frith foresaw that these new tourists would enjoy having souvenirs to commemorate their days out. In 1860 he married Mary Ann Rosling and set out on a new career: his aim was to photograph every city, town and village in Britain. For the next thirty years he travelled the country by train and by pony and trap, producing fine photographs of seaside resorts and beauty spots that were keenly bought by millions of Victorians. These prints were painstakingly pasted into family albums and pored over during the dark nights of winter, rekindling precious memories of summer excursions.

THE RISE OF FRITH & CO

Frith's studio was soon supplying retail shops all over the country. To meet the demand he gathered about him a small team of photographers, and published the work of independent artist-photographers of the calibre of Roger Fenton and Francis Bedford. In order to gain some understanding of the scale of Frith's business one only has to look at the catalogue issued by Frith & Co in 1886: it runs to some 670 pages, listing not only many thousands of views of the British Isles but also many photographs of most European countries, and China, Japan, the USA and Canada - note the sample page shown on page 9 from the hand-written Frith & Co ledgers recording the pictures. By 1890 Frith had created the greatest specialist photographic publishing company in the world, with over 2,000 sales outlets - more than the combined number that Boots and WH Smith have today! The picture on the next page shows the Frith & Co display board at Ingleton in the Yorkshire Dales (left of window). Beautifully constructed with a mahogany frame and gilt inserts, it could display up to a dozen local scenes.

POSTCARD BONANZA

The ever-popular holiday postcard we know today took many years to develop. In 1870 the Post Office issued the first plain cards, with a pre-printed stamp on one face. In 1894 they allowed other publishers' cards to be sent through the mail with an attached adhesive halfpenny stamp. Demand grew rapidly, and in 1895 a new size of postcard was permitted called the court card, but there was little room for illustration. In 1899, a year after Frith's death, a new card measuring 5.5 x 3.5 inches became the standard format, but it was not until 1902 that the divided back came into being, so that the address and message could be on one face and a full-size illustration on the other. Frith & Co were in the vanguard of postcard development: Frith's sons Eustace and Cyril continued their father's monumental task, expanding the number of views offered to the public and recording more and more places in Britain, as the

coasts and countryside were opened up to mass travel.

Francis Frith had died in 1898 at his villa in Cannes, his great project still growing. The archive he created continued in business for another seventy years. By 1970 it contained over a third of a million pictures showing 7,000 British towns and villages.

FRANCIS FRITH'S LEGACY

Frith's legacy to us today is of immense significance and value, for the magnificent archive of evocative photographs he created provides a unique record of change in the cities, towns and villages throughout Britain over a century and more. Frith and his fellow studio photographers revisited locations many times down the years to update their views, compiling for us an enthralling and colourful pageant of British life and character.

We are fortunate that Frith was dedicated to recording the minutiae of everyday life. For it is this sheer wealth of visual data, the painstaking chronicle of changes in dress, transport, street layouts, buildings, housing, engineering and landscape that captivates us so much today. His remarkable images offer us a powerful link with the past and with the lives of our ancestors.

THE VALUE OF THE ARCHIVE TODAY

Computers have now made it possible for Frith's many thousands of images to be accessed almost instantly. Frith's images are increasingly used as visual resources, by social historians, by researchers into genealogy and ancestry, by architects and town planners, and by teachers involved in local history projects.

In addition, the archive offers every one of us an opportunity to examine the places where we and our families have lived and worked down the years. Highly successful in Frith's own era, the archive is now, a century and more on, entering a new phase of popularity. Historians consider the Francis Frith Collection to be of prime national importance. It is the only archive of its kind remaining in private ownership. Francis Frith's archive is now housed in an historic timber barn in the beautiful village of Teffont in Wiltshire. Its founder would not recognize the archive office as it is today. In place of the many thousands of dusty boxes containing glass plate negatives and an all-pervading odour of photographic chemicals, there are now ranks of computer screens. He would be amazed to watch his images travelling round the world at unimaginable speeds through internet lines.

The archive's future is both bright and exciting. Francis Frith, with his unshakeable belief in making photographs available to the greatest number of people, would undoubtedly approve of what is being done today with his lifetime's work. His photographs depicting our shared past are now bringing pleasure and enlightenment to millions around the world a century and more after his death.

SOUTHWOLD TO ALDEBURGH
AN INTRODUCTION

THE TOWNS of Southwold and Aldeburgh and their associated estuaries stand sentinel at either end of a historic coastal strip that invites exploration and never fails to surprise. There is a diversity of scenery and experience here which is remarkable and which draws in a myriad of visitors annually. Crumbling sandy cliffs and shingle beaches, ancient and now rare lowland heaths, creeks of glistening mud, and salt marshes that attract innumerable birds - clearly this is an area of outstanding natural beauty, and it was officially designated as such thirty years ago. Even the looming presence of the Sizewell nuclear power station cannot detract from the visual amenity of this area, and indeed one must admire the courage and confidence of those planners who placed it on Britain's most fragile and vulnerable coast.

Although it can mesmerise with its dramatic beauty, the sea is not always an object of affection here. It has been too fickle a neighbour, bringing food and employment, sometimes lavishly, and then tearing at the land in the most predatory manner. It swept away the great port and town of Dunwich in the Middle Ages, and makes a spiteful attack almost every generation.

Many people still remember the floods of 1953. The capricious sea continues to this day to sustain or to erode the shoreline according to its own rules.

The bustling A12 is the boundary to the west, and it is from this busy artery that you will need to find the B-roads and narrow lanes that will carry you across the heath towards the sea. The charming villages of Westleton and Middleton in the north have successfully resisted the hand of modern man. How do they resist the cold blasts of the eastern wind in winter? Pilgrims today move through them to Dunwich, but not to seek out the great medieval places of worship, one of the gateways of Christianity into England. No, the sea has swallowed them. The pilgrims come rather to experience fish and chips in one of the great eating houses of its type along the east coast - a Suffolk institution, and just a few yards from the sea.

Further south at Theberton and Eastbridge you will need to seek out the footpaths that take you through the Minsmere bird reserves famous nation-wide among 'twitchers'. The nuclear power station looks on quite amiably. Leiston is busier, more closely linked to the Sizewell phenomenon. The great engineering dynasty, the Garretts of Leiston, brought industry and manufacturing here in Victorian times, rivalling even the Ransomes of Ipswich. Today their achievements are remembered in a museum well worth your attention. Finally you will find Saxmundham, now isolated by a grand by-pass road. Ironically, signs encourage you not to drive by but to call in. Saxmundham's existence has depended for a long time on servicing the coaches passing between Lowestoft and Ipswich. Let us hope that the Frith photographs in this volume will encourage a visit. Today new dormitory housing estates point to the town's evolving role, supplying the workforce of Ipswich, Martlesham, and maybe even London at journey's end on the railway.

At the northern end of this diverse area stand Blythburgh and Southwold. Blythburgh owes its earlier importance to its position at the first convenient river crossing on the Blyth. In 1066 it was one of only a dozen market towns in the county, and in the Middle Ages derived benefit as a small trading port. But it is strange that Blythburgh's brush with prosperity had disappeared when the magnificent Holy Trinity Church was being built, a magnificent monument in a bleak marsh setting. Decay set in when the adjoining priory was dissolved by Henry VIII, and the church continued to crumble for centuries, until a magnificent late-Victorian restoration saved it. Today the rushing traffic splits the village, but many stop to marvel at this 'Cathedral of the Marshes', one of the must-visit churches in Suffolk.

Southwold is a town which you cannot discover by chance. Visiting Southwold must be a deliberate act. The rewards for such bravery are substantial. Is there a small town in England more deserving of the attentions of the discerning explorer? Remarkable vistas await around each corner, and civilised greens abound, random dabs of green paint on an already colourful palette.

A solitary old Southwolder quietly reads a magazine in the Sailors' Reading Room, surrounded by the photographic memories, images

WALBERSWICK, *The Green 1919* 69130

and printed memorabilia of a town locked in a battle of centuries with the sea. An uneasy truce seems to exist at the start of the third millennium. There are pictures extant of the sea taking more than its fair share of the town in the great storms of 1906, biting deeply into Gun Hill, for example. The Town Council also had to dig deeply to settle that score - into the pockets of the ratepayers. The delightful small town museum catalogues the wrecks that have fortuitously come ashore, none more famous than the Norwegian barque 'Idun', flung onto the land in 1912. A dramatic rescue of the Viking craft and crew afforded the town no small measure of self-congratulation and well-deserved praise from afar, and locals later enjoyed the economic benefits of a substantial vessel carefully dismantled in situ.

However, the sea can also bring less desirable visitors. At the end of May 1672 a naval fleet of English and French ships, commanded by the King's brother, the Duke of York, perhaps more with an eye to Southwold and its pleasures on land, was attacked by a Dutch fleet led by De Ruyter. On a hot and calm day, the cumbersome vessels moved slowly north - our French allies went south - and a bitter and bloody battle ensued. Perhaps 5,000 men were killed or wounded before the Dutch withdrew, having achieved their aim of surprising and damaging the allied fleets and allied morale. The wounded and some prisoners were put ashore at Southwold, and the fleet retired to the shelter of the Thames. This was the celebrated Battle of Sole Bay.

Today a magnificently restored Victorian pier, utterly Southwold in its uniqueness, draws in the crowds, and the famous beach huts, photographic almost to a fault, give added interest to any walk along the sea-front. It hardly surprises one to read that Monty Python sketches were filmed here, and that there are plans for further radical comedy vignettes. The local brewery is revered among beer drinkers, and the pubs and hotels trade extensively on those visitors who come to share the delights of the sea, the sea in its most hospitable mood.

Leave Southwold, if you must, at its harbour and take the tiny ferry across the Blyth to Walberswick. Keen young crabbers on both sides lower in their bait, but not all have the patience to await a bite. Walberswick has no reminders of its past as a busy ship-building and ship-repairing town, where fishing also brought great wealth in Tudor times. Well, perhaps St Andrew's Church does give a hint of former wealth; but there was a slow and inexorable decline as the community's population shrank.

Thorpeness has the air of a grand Edwardian folly, though it is a little later than that; it is a purpose-built seaside haven. A magnificent lake, the Meare, attracts rowers and ducks alike, and timber-framed houses seize your attention at every juncture. The magnificent House in the Clouds overlooks the village rather sternly. Thorpeness is another of the Suffolk coast's welcome surprises.

And so to Aldeburgh, guardian of the southern boundary of this fascinating corner of England. The moot hall is poised at the edge of the sea, but it was once in the centre of town, reminding us again of how this land seems to live on borrowed time. Today we see a broad high street, safely distant from the crashing waves, and narrow lanes run down to a pebble shore where fishermen sell their freshly caught wares almost from the sterns of their vessels. The lifeboat imperiously waits upon the call.

Aldeburgh is famous for the poet George Crabbe. His poetic masterpiece, 'The Borough', a Suffolk 'Under Milk Wood' in fact, published in 1812, was the inspiration in more modern times for Benjamin Britten's 'Peter Grimes'. Crabbe was admired by his literary contemporaries, and we learn that Jane Austen harboured the fantasy of becoming Mrs Crabbe! He wrote over 40,000 lines of heroic couplets, so many in fact that he helped to kill off the very poetic device itself. His style may have been based on classic Pope and Dryden, but his subjects were alarmingly real and unmistakably modern. He wrote about the men and women he saw in what was then an impoverished and primitive town, far removed from the genteel, prosperous seaside town we enjoy today. The people of Aldeburgh he described as

'... a wild amphibious race,
With sullen woe display'd in every face;
Who far from civil arts and social fly,
And scowl at strangers with suspicious eye'.

Fortunately, the Aldeburgh of today does not reflect Crabbe's cruel vision. The town boasts its restaurants and hotels and many other delights for visitors and residents alike, and is extremely welcoming. The Aldeburgh Festival is one of the most prestigious in Britain, and there is a huge interest here in the visual arts, literature and local history, especially among the retired residents. Benjamin Britten raised the intellectual and artistic profile of Aldeburgh when he chose to make the town his home over half a century ago. His influence lives on, not least through the festival which he founded with some friends.

Fortunate, then, are the residents of this remarkable area where two distinctive towns, Southwold and Aldeburgh, have refused to submit to the excesses and outrages of modern living. Between them and their estuaries, where coastline gives way to countryside, there is a world worthy of your investigation. Indeed, the Frith photographers have captured much of the essential diversity and spirit of these fascinating sandlands.

ALDEBURGH, *The Moot Hall 1894* 33359

SOUTHWOLD

SOUTHWOLD is a town of character and characters; its history, so closely tied to the sea, abounds with glorious adventures, mysteries and disasters, and some extremely fishy tales. 'Hereabouts, they begin to talk of herrings .... and here also they cure sprats in the same manner as they do herrings in Yarmouth', noted the very observant Defoe on his famous perambulation in the early 18th century. Southwold invested furiously in this trade, and herring 'busses', 70-foot square-rigged sailing drifters, brought wealth to the town - but only temporarily. Southwold's harbour was incapable of the kind of expansion which would put it on the same scale as Lowestoft or Great Yarmouth. Now Buss Creek embraces the town on the landward side, a nod to the vessels of old or perhaps a hint of what might have been.

The sea has opened the way for enemy attack, as the Battle of Sole Bay testifies, and at other times has attempted an invasion of the town itself, ripping chunks of cliff away as late as 1906 in spite of solid defensive works. The resilient men and women of Southwold have taken these blows, rebuilt their communities, and reoriented their economic opportunities. Where herrings once brought work and wealth, now tourists are netted in their season, partly salted with walks along the proms or beaches, and sent away restored and refreshed!

The town is worthy of your investigation, and architectural wonders appear around every corner. The carved heads of monarchs stare down at you in one street, the lighthouse monitors your progress throughout, and in the small museum look for the drawings of Southwold cartoonist Reg Carter, an artist with a nation-wide reputation. A town that can laugh at itself must be deserving of your attention.

SOUTHWOLD
The Beach 1896 38620

The crowded beach reminds us of the importance of the sea in the economy of the town and the lives of its inhabitants. The characteristic clinker-built, double-ended beach yawls, the speediest craft on the east coast, competed with each other to off-load cargoes from larger ships offshore. Here sails and also, it seems, fishing nets are drying after a day's work.

SOUTHWOLD
The Beach 1906 56834

A new role for Southwold's beaches emerged in the Victorian era - sea bathing and general leisure use. The town council drew up by-laws to regulate behaviour on the beach, and there were steep fines for misuse of these public places. Here an Edwardian family, impeccably dressed, possibly over-dressed, enjoy a day at the seaside. A nanny, it seems, in the foreground, keeps an eye on things.

SOUTHWOLD, *From the Pier 1919* 69119

Here we see the marriage of bathing machines and fishing boats under the imposing gaze of the Grand Hotel. The hotel, built in 1902, catered for wealthier visitors, who arrived, perhaps, by steamer and landed at the pier itself. However, the hotel's history was less than grand: it never recovered from the indignities of war-time requisition by the army, and was unceremoniously demolished in 1959.

▼ **SOUTHWOLD,** *The Beach 1919* 69110

This is our first look at Southwold Pier, which opened in the summer of 1900. Here the elegant 'Belle' steamers drew alongside, discharging and collecting visitors in what was the glorious era of Edwardian tourism. Like all piers, Southwold underwent many adventures over the years; but today it lives and breathes again as a real attraction for people of all ages and tastes, but especially for those with a sense of fun.

▶ **SOUTHWOLD**
The Pier Entrance c1955 S168032

Not a busy day at the pier; the fluttering flag perhaps indicates why. The pier had been reconstructed after the wartime destruction, but in the year of this Frith visitation an October storm caused severe damage. This was compounded by neglect and further storms until 1999, when the extraordinary story of its rescue began.

◄ **SOUTHWOLD**
East Cliff 1893
32182

An impressive awning protects the entrance of the Southwold Sailors' Reading Room, constructed in 1884 to distract sailors from the evils of strong drink. Patently a number of the members have stepped outside to reminisce in the fresh air. The beach is crowded with boats. Today, beach huts stand safely on a solid prom.

► **SOUTHWOLD**
The Lighthouse and the Coastguard Station 1906 56842

This is St James' Green, site of the old Coastguard Station, which sits under the watchful eye of Southwold's distinctive lighthouse. The central mast was once used for signalling, and two 18th-century guns also stood here at one time. The large building almost shielding the lighthouse has been demolished.

SOUTHWOLD
East Green 45137

The lighthouse inevitably dominates many of the street vistas, not the least of which is East Green. Local tradition claims that the many greens that grace the small town were deliberately planned after the great fire of 1659. The Wesleyan chapel (left) is an intimation of the strong non-conformist tradition in Southwold.

▲ SOUTHWOLD
East Green and the Lighthouse 1933
85869

What a difference a few decades can make. The town council have beautified the green with discreet railed gardens. The Methodists have added a contemporary facade to their chapel. The railings, of course, did not survive the metal drives of World War II.

► *detail from 85869*

SOUTHWOLD, *The Lighthouse c1965* S168208

The Sole Bay Inn stands at the entrance of East Green. The strangely landlocked lighthouse was safely positioned away from the cliff edge but not too central in the town, where the smoke from coal fires might have obscured the light. It was opened in 1890, and stands just over 100ft tall; its light can be seen at sea up to 20 miles away.

SOUTHWOLD
East Street 1919 69123

Now we are walking towards the Market Place. The Lord Nelson (right) has served Southwold faithfully for generations, and is popular with locals and visitors today. A man and child pose cheerfully for the photographer as shoppers go about their business in the background.

▲ SOUTHWOLD
East Street c1955
S168045

We have nearly reached the Market Place in this photograph. Visitors choose postcards from the general store on the left, and one lady waits patiently for the photographer to finish before walking on towards the sea. The sign for the Victoria pub may be identified at the top of the street on the right.

▶ *detail from S168045*

▲ **SOUTHWOLD,** *The Market 1896*
38627

Glance back down East Street towards the sea; there's the Victoria again on the left. It is market day in town, and we do wonder what the vendor is asking for that impressive long-case clock (centre). James Warren's shop, 'the oldest shop in town', has served Southwold since the 1680s. The goat cart in the foreground was a Frith photographer's delight.

◀ *detail from 38627*

SOUTHWOLD
*The Market
Place 1919* 69121

This is an altogether
more busy scene
than it was in 1896
(38627), and newly
emancipated
women boldly walk
in all directions. The
elegant Swan Hotel
dominated the
square, then and
now in fact. A sign
on the right,
'Beware of Motors',
is a warning to
pedestrians to
glance up the
alleyway for cars
emerging between
the hotel and the
Town Hall.

► **SOUTHWOLD**
The Town Hall and High Street c1960
S168087

It is time to look at the cast iron town pump with visual echoes of the lamps gracing London's Victoria embankment. 'Defend thy ryght' is the bold instruction on the pump; above, the diving dolphins look remarkably like Southwold herrings, upon whose bountiful harvest the town relied for centuries.

◄ **SOUTHWOLD**
High Street 1891
28352

Here is a photograph which really rewards a 'then and now' study, though beware today's traffic. Two salty locals (left), now captured in time, look on with no little suspicion. It is not a busy day. The yellow brick imposing structure on the right, with 'Critten 1825' over the door, has served as a chemist's shop under many proprietors over the years.

▲ **SOUTHWOLD,** *The Crown Hotel and High Street c1955* S168027

We are looking back towards the Market Square. The Crown Hotel holds sway in this section of the High Street; its solid-columned portico of Georgian origin tells of an inn which has served the community for a considerable time. The rather obvious sign, 'chemist' (centre), supports our assertion in the caption to photograph 28352 on page 28.

◀ **SOUTHWOLD**
High Street c1955
S168044

Where Victoria Street meets the High Street, we have a busy scene. The post office (second right) is well patronised. The cinema (in the distance, centre left) was soon to be closed, but the imposing furniture shop of James Ward (centre) may still be found, though under new management. Jack O' Lantern's trendy espresso coffee house (right) is now a private garage.
Times change.

SOUTHWOLD
The View from the Lighthouse 1893
32186

This panoramic view shows East Green below and spokes of terraces radiating from the imposing structure of St Edmund's Church and its substantial churchyard. The latter apparently acted as a windbreak during the disastrous fire of 1659, during which hundreds of dwellings and important buildings were destroyed. The church was untouched.

SOUTHWOLD, *The Church of St Edmund from the South-East 1896* 38630

The parish church, dedicated to St Edmund, king and martyr, was completed around 1460. It is an exceptionally fine building fashioned from flint and stone, with an imposing 100ft tower. The south porch is a beautiful structure, light and delicate, with intricate masonry and delightful panels dedicated to the Virgin Mary.

SOUTHWOLD, *Southwold Jack 1893* 32190

Southwold Jack is a rather menacing warrior from the Wars of the Roses. His duty is to strike the bell with his battle-axe upon the pulling of a cord, thus announcing the beginning of services. Today, Jack can be found on the northern arch of the West Tower.

▶ **SOUTHWOLD**
The Green 1896
38624

This is a civilised scene: the range of dwellings beside Southwold's most genteel green disgorges their elegant inmates to take the air, to see and to be seen perhaps. A young lad on a donkey (right) is on an errand, again a blessing to the Frith photographer looking for local colour!

◄ **SOUTHWOLD**
Gunhill 1896
38626

The menacing guns are potent reminders of the danger of unwelcome guests in earlier times, though the uncommunicative pair on the bench seem oblivious to their historical significance. The guns are from the Tudor period, presented to the town in 1746 as a defence against the French. In the two world wars the cannon were buried so as not to annoy the Germans, which seems sensible.

▲ **SOUTHWOLD**
The Coastguard Station 1933
85880

The Coastguard Station stands at the southern end of Gun Hill; here a single officer takes a few moments off from duty to pose for the photograph. The octagonal station had fine views up and down the coast, and was especially important at a time when the Southwold harbour was much busier than today.

▶ *detail from 85880*

SOUTHWOLD
*The Playing Field
1893* 32191

It is the Great Mill, or Black Mill, which is the interesting element of this photograph. This mill had dominated the common for just over 100 years, having been brought down from Yarmouth in 1798. It proudly sits on its new brick roundhouse, catching every gust of wind in its pre-eminent position.

SOUTHWOLD, *The Common 1896* 38629

Southwold Common stands between the town and the marshes, and is lined on its northern edge with a range of private dwellings. Here the photographer has positioned a number of smartly dressed and well-behaved children as artistically as he could; let us hope that their parents are looking on from behind the camera.

► **SOUTHWOLD**
From the Marshes 1896
38633

This is the old salt works. The tripod structure at the head of the creek is the base of a small wind-pump, vital to pump the salt water to the salt pans where the boiling and refining process could take place. The works had closed two years before this picture was taken.

◄**SOUTHWOLD**
The View from the South 1891 28350

Southwold seems to rise out of the marshes. On the right we can see the old salt works, with creeks for holding the briny water while it settled and before the boiling processes were started.

◄ **SOUTHWOLD**
The Harbour Inn
c1955 S168131

There was a time when Southwold hoped to challenge Lowestoft for supremacy in the fishing industry. A major rebuilding programme of the harbour began a hundred years ago, and for a few years before the Great War the herring trade flourished; but it was all a short-lived dream. This view from the Walberswick side, across the River Blyth, shows some activity, including boat repair, chandlery sales and services for visitors.

ALONG THE COAST

IS THERE any part of the British Isles so fundamentally affected by the sea as these vulnerable shores? The bitter east winds have for centuries whipped up the tides to attack the friable and fragile cliffs, carrying away much that was constructed and cherished by man, homes and churches, even whole settlements. Sand and silt deposits have choked harbours and destroyed livelihoods. Walberswick once enjoyed very prosperous times, but the work of nature and of man have left the village a quiet backwater.

The Dunwich story is one of the more remarkable tales in East Anglian history. The Romans had a fortified settlement there, and St Felix used the port as a base from which to bring Christianity to the heathen Saxons. By the time of Domesday, Dunwich was a bustling town, one of the busiest ports in England, a gated town graced by churches, monastic institutions and ship-building yards. An oak forest stood between the town and the sea, much used by noble hunters. A ferocious storm in 1286 tore at the town, and a generation later a further devastation brought ruin. The best efforts of the townspeople could not prevent the almost total demise of Dunwich in the years that followed. Defoe summed it up perfectly when he visited in 1724: 'The town is manifestly decayed by the invasion of the waters'. Tradition states that the bells of the churches lost under the sea may still be heard. Is it possible? Of course it is - on this sea coast of rich imagination.

Thorpeness is an example of man's triumph against the inroads of the sea, a model holiday village with a style of its own, a concept and a community. Frith's photographs capture its uniqueness. Sizewell is today home to one of the wonders of modern technology, yet its beaches were once famous for outrageous smuggling activity. Sometimes goods were brought ashore in broad daylight, and pitched battles with the revenue men made the whole area notorious - but the brandy was cheaper. And as you approach Aldeburgh along the beach, where the land meets the sea, you suddenly become aware of another presence, quite overwhelming, quite simply - the sky. It can be a very pleasing revelation.

WALBERSWICK, *The Ferry 1919* 69126

There has been a ferry across the River Blyth for over 800 years, and between 1885 and 1942 it was the rather primitive chain ferry, which we see here carrying a horse and cart across to the Southwold side. This one is steam-operated. Today, as in the 13th century, a rowing boat provides the service for a modest fee. So, in this case, times do not change!

WALBERSWICK
The Village 1892
29931

This bleak view of the village in the later Victorian period reveals the tidal mud flats beloved mainly by sea birds. The village was awaiting its new role as a haunt for discerning artists and visitors, and that time was near.

WALBERSWICK, *The Bridge and the Village 1900* 45140

A well-worn path indicates a bridge frequently used by the locals. In the distance is a corn-grinding post mill (centre left), possibly owned at this time by a Mr Mallett, whose worry was that the building of houses nearby would keep the wind from the mill's sails. Old age and possibly the fiery enthusiasm of local youths brought the mill to its end shortly after the photograph was taken.

WALBERSWICK
The Village 1919 69128

This is a much more civilised image of Walberswick. The pub and the tea room (right) point to the village's new role. A trader is about to make a sale, but he will not make a fortune from this cart unless all of Walberswick turns out.

WALBERSWICK
The Green 1919
69130

A young lad offers advice to his dad, who appears to be working under the car in the tiny lay-by on the left. His sister hardly had to be persuaded to show off her new bicycle (centre). Behind, a wide green stretches out. It was this simplicity and quiet which had recently attracted the architect and painter Charles Rennie Mackintosh to stay and work.

WALBERSWICK, *The Green c1965* W7082

Little has changed in the 40 years since photograph 69130 was taken, although there is a strong hint of things to come with the slow intrusion of the motor car. Rogers & Son (left) offer petrol sales and repairs, and next door a pottery shop caters essentially for visitors.

WALBERSWICK
The Church 1891
28355

Here is a building that speaks history, the story of Walberswick's decline. This church is a sister church to Blythburgh, both completed at the end of the 15th century. But as Walberswick declined, so the building retreated, and no one came forward to save it as Blythburgh was saved. Now a smaller building stands within the ruins of a more prosperous era.

DUNWICH, *The Beach 1909* 62044

A substantial shingle beach this may be, but it offers no protection to the sandy cliffs. All Saints' Church now stands at the edge, soon to join the lost medieval town in a watery grave. In recent years, divers have probed the sea bed and located ruins in the murky deep.

▶ **DUNWICH**
The Village
c1955 D173003

Youngsters
return from the
beach, seemingly
with plenty of
energy left. This
is a holiday
village, and
popular too with
day trippers from
the small Suffolk
inland towns, but
bleak in winter.
One pub remains
- the Ship, seen
on the left.

◀ **DUNWICH**
St James' Church
1891 28358

One small church
survives to look after the
spiritual needs of the
village. The remains of
the old leper hospital
may be located in the
churchyard, and also a
buttress from All Saints',
the last surviving stones
of that great building,
rescued from the cliff
edge.

▲ **DUNWICH,** *The Church Ruins 1891* 28359

What weddings and baptisms brought joy to the community from within these walls of All Saints' in olden times? Now the sad remains await the final indignity, as the sea completes its task of 700 years and claims the last monuments of a once great town.

◄**DUNWICH**
The Ship Hotel c1965
D173078

The Ship now stands alone; the ugly garages we saw in photograph D173003 (page 44) have been removed in the previous ten years. A small and prize-winning museum is today found at the end of the terrace on the left. Strange to think that up to 1832 the 'town' of Dunwich sent two MPs to the House of Commons.

THORPENESS

THORPENESS is testament to the determination of man to defy the elements and construct a settlement which embraces the best that the sea has to offer. In 1903 a parish called Aldringham-cum-Thorpe, with its pub and scattered houses, came under the ownership of one Glencairn Stuart Ogilvie, an author and man of considerable artistic vision, whose dream was to create a holiday village for discerning visitors. When the Meare flooded in 1910 Ogilvie ingeniously saw it as the centre of his project, and a shallow and safe lake was created. Half-timbered mock-Tudor houses appeared around it in the years that followed, and in 1919 the estate was officially graced with the name Thorpeness.

THORPENESS, *The Boat House 1922* 72589

The Boat House was built in 1911, one of the first structures in Ogilvie's fantasy community, and the Meare can just be spotted behind it. The Tudor-style timbering of the nearby buildings was the architectural theme of this 20th-century wonderworld.

THORPENESS
The Lake 1922
72591

A small trick of nature started the Thorpeness dream. Flooding in 1910 created a vast temporary lake, which Stuart Ogilvie realised would make a centre-piece to his village. Eventually the Meare, as it is more correctly called, covered an area of 64 acres, with magical islands to explore and shallow water for absolute safety.

THORPENESS, *The Estate Office c1955* T38018

The Estate Office was built in 1925, and was originally known as Barn Hall. The estate was a considerable economic undertaking, requiring management of the holiday facility and planning for the growth and development of the village. Here the decisions were made. A pony and trap pass by on the sandy path.

▼ **THORPENESS,** *The Dunes Guesthouse 1929* 82983

This is one of the southernmost buildings in the old village, and was completed just before the outbreak of war in 1914. It was still a guesthouse when the photograph was taken, and catered for the wealthier classes.

► **THORPENESS**
The Sanctuary 1929
82984

The building on the left has strong echoes of the Moot Hall in Aldeburgh. Before you stands the impressive, almost outrageous tower and archway of the almshouse building, designed by W G Wilson, which served the staff of the Ogilvie Estate and was not strictly part of the holiday complex.

The House in the Clouds and the Windmill c1955
T38012

This most elegant post mill, originally a corn grinding mill, used to stand in nearby Aldringham. It was moved in 1923 to serve a different purpose - to pump water to the huge tank serving Thorpeness, so beautifully disguised as the House in the Clouds. Only in Suffolk could this happen!

▶ **THORPENESS**
The Benthills 1929
82979

We are looking along the Benthills road towards Aldeburgh. A variety of impressive cars have parked, possibly marking the advent of day trippers, which Ogilvie did not really want. At one stage the residents of Benthills enjoyed exclusive use of the beach area in front of their houses - 'The Benthills Enclosure'.

▶ THORPENESS
From the Beach c1960
T38047

These rather ugly garden sheds do not have the glamour of a Southwold beach hut, and were not guaranteed to withstand the sharp eastern blasts. Above, the more elegant houses look down on the beach and out to sea. Today the Ogilvie holiday village dream is no more, and Thorpeness is home to many permanent residents.

▼ *detail from 82982*

The Beach 1929
82982

But before we lose
the romance of
G S Ogilvie's glorious
concept, here is one
last glance up the
beach. Sturdy
fishermen's boats
offer shelter to the
visitors, and many
brave souls are
tempted into the
water.

INLAND TOWNS AND VILLAGES

WE MUST NOT become too enthralled with the sea and the excitements of coastal villages and small towns. Small towns like Saxmundham and Leiston and villages such as Middleton and Westleton speak of a different life, involved in the diverse world of agriculture.

Saxmundham and Leiston both claim a Saxon heritage. Certainly the former of these was a substantial settlement by the time of Domesday Book, and enjoyed market rights in the Middle Ages. It was at the centre of the farming community for centuries with regular livestock markets. The railway arrived in 1859, and included a branch line to Aldeburgh. However, one associates Saxmundham with the old turnpike and the modern A12, and here the Bell Inn could tell some tales from all the travellers who have rested there. Today the by-pass, long fought for, has brought the town a measure of peace and quiet, especially from those rumbling monsters of the road, trucks and lorries. It is ironic, perhaps, that its convenience has prompted a house-building programme, so that the population of Saxmundham has risen above

4000. A strong sense of small-town community spirit seems to exist there, we are happy to say.

Leiston owes its medieval prosperity to a substantial abbey which flourished up to the Dissolution in 1537. In the 19th century, the firm of Garretts dominated the town, and the manufactures of the company, including formidable steam engines of all kinds, were sold world wide. We must not forget that Suffolk played an important part in the early and developing Industrial Revolution. Today a fascinating museum records the triumphs of Garretts of Leiston. In the 1950s, a nuclear power station was commissioned, a Magnox reactor of formidable potential, bringing new employment opportunities. Later came Sizewell B, the PWR reactor, proudly state-of-the-art; today the giant white dome stands rather incongruously where smugglers once plied a profitable trade.

Both towns claim to be the hub of this Area of Outstanding Natural Beauty, and indeed they are both useful starting points for a journey of exploration in such a special place.

BLYTHBURGH, *The Village c1955* B125004

Like Snape, Blythburgh stands on a key part of its river, the Blyth, where navigation effectively comes to an end. Since the decline of coal, grain and malt wherries and the end of 50 years of railway in 1929, the village is dependent on road traffic. S Harrison Ade's 'High Class Stores' reflects the reliance upon well-stocked local shops in the post-war period.

BLYTHBURGH
The Church 1895
36879

This magnificent church, 'the Cathedral of the Marshes', is a testament to the agricultural and maritime riches of coastal Suffolk in the 15th century. Its size, extensive stained glass, long since depleted, and exquisite carvings reflect the ambition and power of rich individuals seeking salvation in the late medieval period.

BLYTHBURGH, *The Church and the Village 1895* 36881

As the photograph clearly illustrates, the church was gloriously over-sized and over-opulent for an area dependent on butter, cheese and a little fishing. Physical decline of the church's fabric began as early as the 16th century and accelerated through periods of poverty, damage and indifference. The gentle ministrations of 20th-century restorers have created an ambience of stunning light and simplicity.

WESTLETON
The Village c1950
W441008

Old England can still be found in villages like these, and even today Westleton is a delight to explore, with church and green and very particular ducks on the pond. We are looking across one of the greens towards the war memorial and the old elementary school.

WESTLETON
The White Horse
c1950 W441003

Ah, the village pub! And proudly below the gable end, with its hint of Dutch style, are the words that mean so much to locals: 'Adnams, Southwold Ales'. Adnams is a great Southwold institution, and served pubs like these across the county. It is a strange fact that the beer seems to taste better the closer you get to the brewery!

WESTLETON, *The Green c1950* W441005

We are looking back towards the view of the village we see in W441008 (page 54-55). The village store on the right was enjoying its last days of prosperity, with the end of rationing and before the onset of superstores. The little chapel just visible on the right is now a rather fascinating book shop, crowded with ancient treasures.

WESTLETON
The Mill c1950
W441006

The village enjoyed two mills at one time. This is a late 18th-century smock mill, sometimes called Ralph's Mill. Its sails were long gone when this photograph was taken, and the tower was finally demolished in 1969.

WESTLETON, *The Green c1950* W441002

This post mill dates from the 1840s; until its demolition in 1963, it overlooked and graced the green.

SAXMUNDHAM
The Village 1929 82947

The Frith photographer was less than kind with his description of Saxmundham as a village. The Bell Hotel (right) was an ancient coaching inn from turnpike days, but was gloriously rebuilt in 1842, as is evident in this photograph. The history of the Bell Hotel needs a substantial volume, but it is interesting to note that in 1737 George II called in. Call in today, and you may just hear the ghosts of the American air crews noisily celebrating successful missions in times past.

► **SAXMUNDHAM**
The High Street
c1955 S69009

These are the last
days of post-war
quiet. This was still
the main highway
between Ipswich and
Lowestoft. Shoppers
park outside the
shops or the pub in
the centre. The range
of architectural styles
is wide but
harmonious.

◄ **SAXMUNDHAM**
The Woodbridge
Road 1929 82948

We leave Saxmundham
on the road towards
Woodbridge. The bold
facade of the wine
merchant's (centre)
impresses, and in fact it
still does to this day. The
great by-pass road has
restored some
tranquillity to
Saxmundham today, but
Frith's idyllic scene will
never quite be repeated.

▲ LEISTON, *High Street 1922* 72577

The rather smart youngsters show no reaction to the news of the 'new crisis' on the newspaper placard on the left: the Germans had defaulted on their reparations payments. Such news seems out of place and irrelevant in a street of elegant Victorian villas in a small town in rural Suffolk.

◄**LEISTON**
High Street 1922 72579

Awnings are out on the sunny side of the street, and the long shadows point to the end of the afternoon. The children are just out of school. Locals bought their shoes at Freeman Hardy & Willis (right), we note.

▶ **LEISTON**
High Street c1955
L33032

There's something for everybody here on the High Street: a stationers, china and glass, the chemist's shop and the opticians. It seems likely that many of these proprietors lived above their shops too.

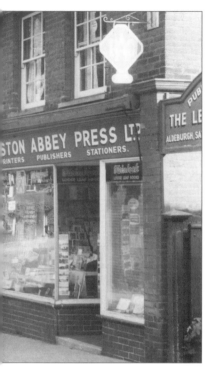

▲ detail of L33032

◀ **SIZEWELL**
The Nuclear Power Station
c1965 S582039

Sizewell has been part of Suffolk life for
half a century, and now seems part of
the coastal landscape, visible for miles
up and down the shore. A two-year
enquiry was held at the Snape Maltings
to prepare for Sizewell B. These
modern power generators bring
massive employment to the area,
including 40,000 visitors annually.

◄ **SNAPE**
The Green c1955
S585007

◄ SNAPE
The Cross c1955 S585006

The Frith photographer did not pause long at Snape on that clear summer's day in 1955. He found a quiet village with almost no human interest, and he moved on to Aldeburgh. Snape, however, is at the end of the navigable River Alde, and certainly in living memory cargoes have unloaded grain for the Maltings. Snape has undergone considerable changes in the last half-century. In 1967 the Queen opened a concert hall carved out of the old industrial buildings, and in phoenix-like fashion it rose again after a disastrous fire. Today the Aldeburgh Festival draws in artists and visitors from across the world to play and enjoy music of the highest quality, a wonderful tribute to co-founder of the Festival, Benjamin Britten, whose music is so evocative of the Suffolk shore. Antique shops and art galleries now vie for your attention in the buildings that crowd around the Maltings, and outside there is a blend of sculpture and nature. Tearooms and a fine pub cater for those in need of refreshment.

◄ SNAPE
The Village c1955
S585009

ALDEBURGH

HOW pleasing to end this visual and historical journey at Aldeburgh.

'During the present century the town has considerably improved; its salubrious air and extensive beach on which there is a splendid walk of nearly two miles, having induced many families to make it their summer residence, several mansions and villa residences have sprung up with three commodious hotels. From the hill behind the town there is a splendid view of the German ocean.'

This was how Morris & Co's Directory viewed Aldeburgh in 1868. Certainly the town was enjoying a revival of fortune, for Crabbe's Aldeburgh of sixty years before was plainly undistinguished. The Regency fashion for sea bathing was the start of Aldeburgh's improved outlook. When Morris was writing, the railway had reached the town, and it helped to sustain the economy for century. We must not forget that there were still nearly 200 licensed fishing vessels in Aldeburgh at this time, catching herrings and sprats and sole. Between these working boats sprawled on the shingle, bathing huts were appearing; and as the Frith photographs show, the two trades lived peacefully together.

Certain personalities moulded the town in its modern history. Newson Garrett was one, and the profits from his entrepreneurial skill helped to reshape Aldeburgh. He built the Jubilee Hall to celebrate Victoria's long reign, and later Benjamin Britten used the hall extensively in the first years of the now internationally-known Aldeburgh Festival. There are distinguished women too in the Aldeburgh story. Elizabeth Garrett Anderson, Newson's second daughter, fought tenaciously for the right to qualify as a doctor. She succeeded, and later broke down another barrier when she became the first woman in Britain to hold the office of Mayor - of Aldeburgh, of course. She is a key figure in the achievement of women's rights.

Like Southwold, there is a tale around almost every corner in Aldeburgh, and the images of the Frith photographers take on a special significance in helping us start to explore and understand the history and life of this small town on the edge of the sea.

ALDEBURGH, *Church Hill 1903* 50437

The entrance to Aldeburgh looks less than appealing on this autumnal day. The parish church of St Peter and St Paul stands on the hill. The spacious interior was used for ship auctions, and also accommodated the entertainments of strolling players in Tudor and Stuart times.

ALDEBURGH
The Lifeboat Men's Memorial 1903 50439

The sacrifice made by seven brave seamen is noted in this simple but striking memorial. In 1899 the lifeboat 'Aldeburgh' foundered in heavy seas. A local appeal raised funds for the dependants and for the construction of the monument.

ALDEBURGH, *Victoria Road c1955* A28015

Below Church Hill and the main street, Victoria Road provides us with our first glimpse of the sea and of the Moot Hall. The well-established hostelry the Windmill (centre) is still flourishing, though not the Cross Hotel (left).

▼ **ALDEBURGH,** *Crabbe Street c1955* A28096

We are looking north along Crabbe Street, which in the mid 1950s was a peaceful backwater dotted with classic cars of that period. The attractive pitched roofline of the Olde Cross Keys Inn (right) can still be admired today.

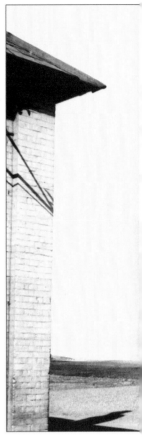

► **ALDEBURGH**
The Moot Hall
1906 56822

One could not find a more quintessentially salty character than the fellow in the foreground, now visually preserved for all time. He is staring out to sea. There is another goat cart here, so beloved by the Frith photographers, to the left of the Moot Hall.

◀ **ALDEBURGH**
The Moot Hall
1894 33360

Built in 1540, during the post-moot age really, this red brick and half-timbered Moot Hall would have been a hotbed of commercial and legal activities during the town's most prosperous era. It has also served as a police station and a jail. It is the symbol of Aldeburgh. Today it houses a fine museum display.

▶ **ALDEBURGH**
The Moot Hall
1894 33359

Little more than a shingle beach protects the Moot Hall. Once it was centrally placed in the town, but the sea has carried away a number of streets, finally pausing here. At the nearby White Lion (centre right), a carriage delivers guests.

ALDEBURGH
The Children's Boating Pool and the Moot Hall c1955 A28062

Here we have a gentle scene. Youngsters enjoy the boating pool: so this is where they first learn the art of sailing, just a stone's throw from the shore line where full-scale vessels sit, awaiting their time to sail.

▲ **ALDEBURGH**
The Beach 1906 56817

Almost everyone wears a hat; some are
extremely stylish. Here we also see how
easily boats can be launched off the
shingle. The shadows seem to indicate
that the time is midday - perhaps
afternoon fishing trips are planned.

► *detail from 56817*

▲ **ALDEBURGH**
The Parade 1909 62011

A flimsy wall protects these stately villas from the sea. A proud dad, a sailor home from the sea, takes his daughter for a stroll along the very sandy path, and a rather bored pony meanders towards the camera.

◀ *detail from 62011*

ALDEBURGH
Crag Path c1960
A28145

A half century has passed since photograph 62011 was taken, and hurrah! a more solid wall protects the town. The esplanade is dominated visually by two look-out towers - this one is the southern lookout. Rival companies manned these towers to pick up the lucrative pilot trade into the Thames Estuary.

ALDEBURGH, *The Parade 1906* 56816

We are looking north at the North Lookout. C Harling catered for those visitors looking for the delights of bathing and boating, and the advertisement on his hut (right foreground) suggests that 'Holloway's Pills and Ointment are family blessings'. It would be churlish to disagree.

ALDEBURGH
The Esplanade 1896
38668

This is a quiet scene. We can see the South Lookout again. The two rival companies mentioned before, who manned the towers, were nicknamed 'Up-Towners' and 'Down-Towners'; they raced to supply pilots and land cargoes, almost running errands to the passing ships. Then there was the bounty of salvage as the stormy seas battered vessels into submission.

ALDEBURGH, *The Lifeboat and Crag Path c1965* A28143

Life-saving eventually took precedence over salvage, and here the lifeboat 'The Alfred and Patience Cottwald' waits for the call, staring silently out towards the waves. This very poignant scene does not require words of explanation to anyone who has lived near the sea.

ALDEBURGH
The Lifeboat
'Winchester' 1903
50426

There is a justifiable pride
in being a lifeboat man.
Here coxswain James Cable
and his men proudly show
off 'The City of Winchester',
presented by that city, a
replacement for the
'Aldeburgh' so tragically lost
a few years before. This boat
served until 1928 and saved
forty lives.

▶ ALDEBURGH
The Beach 1929
82969

Were bathing machines (right) being used as late as 1929? They must have been useful as changing huts, but surely not to make sea-bathing discreet and private, as in Victorian times. Beach furniture includes the winding gear that helped to pull boats onto the shingle (centre).

◀ ALDEBURGH
*The Fishing Boats
c1955* A28048

Something really fascinates a crowd of very curious beach-goers - not just a landing of fish. We will never know what it was! The couple in the foreground are conspicuously lacking in interest, however. Thorpeness is just visible to the north.

▲ **ALDEBURGH,** *The Esplanade 1894* 33355

Such open spaces as you see on the right provided room to dry and certainly to repair nets. The beach is covered with the detritus of the fishing trade - barrels, boxes and buckets, neatly juxtaposed with bathing machines for the hardy swimmers.

◄ **ALDEBURGH**
Pretoria Terrace 1903
50435

Let us leave the sea for a while. Pretoria Terrace, a well-rutted mud and sand road, looks towards the town steps. The name of the terrace must commemorate the recently fought Boer War. Today, this is Park Lane, almost unchanged except for the inevitable loss of those decorative iron railings.

ALDEBURGH, *The Town Steps c1960* A28088

The steps are still well used, carrying pedestrians, locals and explorers from the High Street to the residential area above. There seems to be considerable socialising half way up in this photograph.

ALDEBURGH
The Town Steps 1906
56826

We are looking down from the upper level of the town, which was constructed mainly in the last decades of the Victorian era. Newson Garrett is associated with much of the development here; he was a mighty influence upon Aldeburgh on the architectural front, but his two daughters, Elizabeth Garrett Anderson and Millicent Garrett Fawcett, had an even greater influence on British society.

ALDEBURGH, *High Street 1894* 33362

Frith's photographers visited Aldeburgh's High Street over a period of sixty years; their photographs, arranged here in chronological order, are a potent record of changing times, the advance of the motor car and the fluctuations of the retail trade. The street endures, but how we use it is subject to the fortunes of the age, our evolving priorities, and the search for economic opportunity. This first view shows a remarkably deserted High Street, with evidence of horse-drawn transport. There are impressive gas lights, art nouveau in style, on the left-hand side. The shop awnings give shade from the late afternoon sunshine.

▼ **ALDEBURGH,** *High Street 1896* 38666

A similar view to 33362, looking towards the old market square two years later, highlights the range of architecture in this fine ancient thoroughfare. The imposing building in the left foreground is the Circulating Library, which catered for the reading requirements of an increasingly well-educated public.

► **ALDEBURGH**
High Street 1909
62009

This view just after the turn of the century shows the enduring use of horse power and the emergence of the bicycle too. Aldeburgh at this time was unique in being the only borough in England to boast a female mayor - the distinguished, and first, female Doctor of Medicine, Elizabeth Garrett Anderson.

◀ **ALDEBURGH**
*The Old
Market Square
1929* 82977

By 1929 the road
surface of the
High Street had
been improved
dramatically to
accommodate
motorised
transport. Here,
the bus arrives in
town; a range of
vans have found
a parking place,
forming their
own traffic island.
A motorcycle
make its way out
of the square.

▶ **ALDEBURGH**
High Street c1955
A28095

The High Street is even
busier by the mid-
century, reflecting the
growth of service
industries in
Aldeburgh and the
gradual return to
prosperity after World
War II. And yes,
Aldeburgh is also
famous for its fish and
chips (left). The East
Suffolk Hotel (the
white building, centre)
now houses tourist
information and an
art gallery.

ALDEBURGH
The Red House, the Home of Benjamin Britten c1960
A28126

'I belong at home - there, in Aldeburgh', said Benjamin Britten, certainly one of our great composers. He had lived for a while in Crabbe Street, but moved to the Red House in 1957 to escape the intrusion of the public gaze.
He died in this house in 1976.

ALDEBURGH, *The River Alde 1901* 46709

A crowded rowing boat makes its way to the muddy shore. Stretching away to the south is the Alde, passing the Martello Tower on its left; it runs adjacent to the shore for a further ten miles, a quite remarkable feat considering that the sometimes violent sea is so close.

ALDEBURGH
*Slaughden Quay
1906* 56821

Slaughden was once an important ship building port, but as the Alde silted up so the industry declined. Smaller fishing vessels and beach yawls continued to be built there in more recent times. At its prime Slaughden was well populated, with homes, warehouses and a pub. Here boats lie asleep in the perfectly still waters.

ALDEBURGH, *The Martello Tower c1960* A28100

This is the last and most northerly of just over a hundred Martello towers, built to keep Napoleon at bay. This one was constructed well after the invasion threat. The tide is high, and we can see how over the years it has eaten at the solid protective moat surrounding the tower. Behind us stretches a shingle bank down to Orford and beyond, where the Alde meets the sea.

ALDEBURGH
The Old 'Ionia' 1952 A28001

The 'Ionia' was a wooden fishing smack built in
Grimsby in 1872 and set up on the Slaughden
saltings as a houseboat. It has in its time even
been a holiday home for orphan girls. By the
mid 1960s its parlous state was giving concern,
and it was destroyed by fire in 1974.

ALDEBURGH, *Slaughden 1906* 56820

Here we see a tangled web of wood and rope in a photograph evoking the end of an era. Almost in the memory of this young lad, the sea had competed its final devastation of Slaughden. Today an active yacht club with a prestigious club house brings activity to this creek.

INDEX

NAMES OF SUBSCRIBERS

The following people have kindly supported this book by subscribing to copies before publication.

Mr & Mrs F Bartholomew

Mrs Ann Bicker (formerly Reydon)

Charles D D Boswell

Ms Ceinwen Bridewell, Aldeburgh

The Brown Family

Mr W Burgess

Ken Burton

Mr D E & Mrs M D Clayton Remembered

Peter & Jenny Cooch, Gt Brignton & Aldeburgh

Gordon M Cosgrove, Leiston

Reg Coxage, Saxmundham

Susan M Day - In memory of Mother & Father

Mr P & Mrs J L Fairchild

To my Mum, Debra Flannigan

F Fletcher

Emma & Daniel Goddard, Leiston

Mr W & Mrs L Goddard, Leiston

Pamela & Richard Goodchild

Jill, John, Georgia & Daisy Gray, Wilts

Christopher Haddon from Saxmundham

L P Herrington & Family, Southwold

P J Howard-Dobson

In Memory of John Robert Harvey Humphreys

Betty Hutching's Family, Aldeburgh

Peter & Sheila Jones

Mr & Mrs A J Keeble, Aldeburgh

M E Kingham, Earl Soham

Peter G Lloyd, Leiston

Mr M P Lucas

Mr & Mrs Manning

John & Teresa Martin, Snape, Suffolk

Geoffrey & Sheila Meadows, Knodishall

T P Moore

P F Noble

John F Parsons

Michael Paul

Chris Ramsey - Memories of Eastbridge

The Richardson Family

Michael Roper, Naseby & Aldeburgh

John & Susie Smith

In memory of Majorie 'Babs' Smith, Leiston

R L Smith

Mr & Mrs Sutherland

The Sylvester/Pritt Family, Rickmansworth

F Taylor

John A Triggs

Audrey Turner & family

Gordon Margret Wigg

Jean & Gordon Wigg, Leiston

Mr & Mrs Edward Wild

Mr E R Wood

FRITH PRODUCTS & SERVICES

Francis Frith would doubtless be pleased to know that the pioneering publishing venture he started in 1860 still continues today. Over a hundred and forty years later, The Francis Frith Collection continues in the same innovative tradition and is now one of the foremost publishers of vintage photographs in the world. Some of the current activities include:

Interior Decoration

Today Frith's photographs can be seen framed and as giant wall murals in thousands of pubs, restaurants, hotels, banks, retail stores and other public buildings throughout the country. In every case they enhance the unique local atmosphere of the places they depict and provide reminders of gentler days in an increasingly busy and frenetic world.

Product Promotions

Frith products are used by many major companies to promote the sales of their own products or to reinforce their own history and heritage. Frith promotions have been used by Hovis bread, Courage beers, Scots Porage Oats, Colman's mustard, Cadbury's foods, Mellow Birds coffee, Dunhill pipe tobacco, Guinness, and Bulmer's Cider.

Genealogy and Family History

As the interest in family history and roots grows world-wide, more and more people are turning to Frith's photographs of Great Britain for images of the towns, villages and streets where their ancestors lived; and, of course, photographs of the churches and chapels where their ancestors were christened, married and buried are an essential part of every genealogy tree and family album.

Frith Products

All Frith photographs are available Framed or just as Mounted Prints and Posters (size 23 x 16 inches). These may be ordered from the address below. From time to time other products - Address Books, Calendars, Table Mats, etc - are available.

The Internet

Already fifty thousand Frith photographs can be viewed and purchased on the internet through the Frith websites and a myriad of partner sites.

For more detailed information on Frith companies and products, look at these sites:

www.francisfrith.co.uk
www.francisfrith.com
(for North American visitors)

See the complete list of Frith Books at:
www.francisfrith.co.uk
This web site is regularly updated with the latest list of publications from the Frith Book Company. If you wish to buy books relating to another part of the country that your local bookshop does not stock, you may purchase on-line.

For further information, trade, or author enquiries please contact us at the address below:
The Francis Frith Collection, Frith's Barn, Teffont, Salisbury, Wiltshire, England SP3 5QP.
Tel: +44 (0)1722 716 376 Fax: +44 (0)1722 716 881 Email: sales@francisfrith.co.uk

See Frith books on the internet at www.francisfrith.co.uk